My Body Is a Gift from God

Introducing Conversations to Safeguard Children

Sherie Adams Christensen, MFT

Illustrated by Kamryn Brockbank

To my precious children.
This was always about you in the first place. —SAC

To ice cream, chocolate, and my amazing parents.
Without any of them I would never have made it this far. —KB

Acknowledgments

As a therapist working with sex addicts and their families, I began noticing a disconcerting pattern. Though our society is becoming more and more sexualized, we are not seeing a corresponding trend in parent-child communication about healthy sexuality. Most parents I talk to know their children are at risk. They know they need to talk to their children frequently. But they have no idea how. The fear of doing something wrong, or of arousing curiosity and experimentation, paralyzes them. And as a result, children are left to their own devices to obtain information.

I saw the great need for educating, not children, but their parents. I began presenting. The response was overwhelming. Parents asked me to write what I was teaching. I wrote several chapters of a book for parents. Then I had the idea for this book. I sat down and wrote the first draft with the help of a good friend, Marci McPhee. Life circumstances prevented me from completing either project. I am indebted to Marci for continuing to remind me of their importance, and of relying on God's timing when I felt discouraged. Seven years later the doors suddenly opened and I felt God's timing was right. Since then I have made wonderful connections and received help from many who have moved this book quickly along. I am grateful to Kristen Jensen whose knowledge about entering the world of authoring has been invaluable. Thank you to my amazing illustrator, Kamryn Brockbank, who learned with me and put up with my innumerable revisions. A big thanks to my interior book designer and logo designer, Meggan Hayes, and to all those in focus groups and otherwise who gave me such fabulous feedback.

And finally, thank you to my family. My mother was an incredible support, my children put up with my absence, and my husband was an amazing sounding board and cheerleader... and picked up a lot of balls I dropped while focusing on this book.

Disclaimer

While I am a therapist, I am not your therapist. This book is not intended as a diagnosis or as treatment. If you are in need of either, please make an appointment with a qualified professional.

Sherie Adams Christensen, MFT

Sherie Adams Christensen has a Masters Degree in Marriage and Family Therapy. She has worked with sex addicts and their families for twelve years both clinically and on a volunteer basis. Her passion is teaching parents how to have healthy sexuality conversations with their children, and she is currently writing a chapter book for parents on the topic. Sherie has presented across the United States and internationally. She loves triathlons, music, nature, reading, and most especially her 4 children and husband.

Kamryn Brockbank

Kamryn Brockbank has been drawing since she was two. Her parents found a doodle and both thought the other parent had drawn it until they caught Kamryn in the act. This is her first publication. Kamryn is entering her senior year of high school. She hopes to continue her career in art as an animator. In her spare time she loves performing in theatre productions and singing in a Madrigal group.

Parent Preface

You try to be vigilant, but it's simply impossible to completely prevent your child's exposure to sexual content in the media and in life. Unexpected situations on handheld devices, TV, in the grocery store checkout line, or on the playground can be harmful or even dangerous without parental guidance and support.

You can preempt the negative consequences of that exposure and protect your child from additional harm. But how do you educate your children on sexual topics—according to your values—without frightening them or damaging their innocence? You begin with foundational, age-appropriate language. Language that allows comfortable dialogue around sexual topics. Language that fits within and promotes your values. Language that, if used consistently, will help your child develop a positive self-image, skills to discern and maintain healthy interactions, and joy in their miraculous body.

This book provides that language in the emotionally safe setting of reading together. Notice how it helps you and your children easily converse about sexual topics. Potentially difficult topics such as body image, healthy relationships, sexual abuse, pornography, and sexual peer pressure become accessible for young ages.

Ideally, regular conversations would begin before a child's first exposure to sexual content. Statistically, this means beginning age-appropriate conversations in the preschool years. But if your children are older, don't worry. Just start now! Children will grasp this language at their current level of understanding and life experiences, and comprehend deeper meanings as they mature.

Parents often have intuition and impressions about the specific needs of their children. The language presented in this book helps you turn intuition into conversations. Whenever these impressions come to mind, make comments. Ask questions. Use this language to begin a regular, healthy, and supportive dialogue. Rather than being difficult and awkward, these talks will deepen your relationship with and ultimately help protect your child.

God loves me so much He gave me a special gift—

my body!

I've lived in my body
my whole life.

I can do wonderful things with my body.

I can **move** with my body.

I can
learn
with my body.

I can
explore
with my body.

I can
feel
with my body.

Because my body is a special gift,

I keep my body
clean.

I eat
healthy
foods.

I take good care of it.

I get plenty of
sleep.

I
exercise.

7

Another way to take good care
of my body is by being modest.

Being modest means
I respect my body
and others' bodies.

It means I treat bodies like
heavenly gifts that help each of
us be the best we can be.

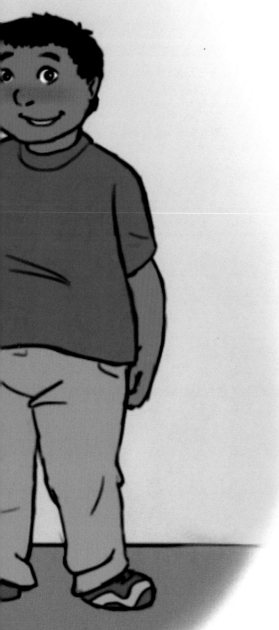

I choose to be modest when I **appreciate that each person's body is different.**

These differences help make each of us **wonderful.**

I choose to be modest when I
speak respectfully about bodies.

I choose to be modest when I
think respectful thoughts
about bodies.

I choose to be modest when I
put down books and magazines right
away when what they say or show
is not modest.

I choose to be modest when I turn off music, the TV, handheld devices, phones, or the computer right away when what they say or show is not modest.

I choose to be modest by

looking away, or leaving, if others choose
not to be modest.

I choose to be modest by

asking others before I touch, hug, or kiss them. I also get to choose who touches, hugs, or kisses me.

I choose to be modest in how I dress.

Modest clothing is about respecting my body
and inviting respect for the
person I am inside.
Modest clothing is appropriate for the
activity I am doing.
My parents help me know what clothing is
modest for me.

The parts of my body that my swimsuit covers up are very special.

I choose to be modest when I don't let others see or touch those special parts of my body, unless my mom or dad says it is okay, like when I am at the doctor's office for a checkup.

If someone tries to do something to my body
that isn't modest, or show me things that
aren't modest, I do my best to leave
—even if I have to yell or run!
And I always tell my mom or dad right away,
especially if I am told not to.

They protect me and will never
be mad at me. They know what
other people choose to do is not
my fault.

I talk to my parents about the things I see,
hear, or do. Sometimes those things are modest.
Sometimes they are not. Sometimes I am not sure but
I still feel uncomfortable.
My parents help me figure it out.

Sometimes it might seem hard to talk to my parents, but I choose to be brave and talk to them anyway.

I always feel a lot better after I talk to my parents because my parents and God still love me if I accidentally see or hear things that are not modest. They even love me when I make mistakes. Making mistakes and fixing them is part of figuring things out and growing up.

God has given me a special
and wonderful body.

I like to take good
care of my body.

I feel happy when I choose to be modest because His Spirit is with me.

God is happy when I honor Him by taking care of my body and choosing to be modest.

Follow-up Discussions:

What are some things you have heard others say (or "things you have said") that were not modest?

A discussion can follow about why that language is not modest. Younger children may need prompts of situations you've observed.

Is modesty about me or somebody else?

"Modesty is about me!" First, it's important to teach the difference between taking responsibility for your choices and judging other people for their choices: "If others are making different choices, or have different values than you, does that make them bad? No. Does it make us bad that we make different choices, or have different values, than they do? No." Second, separating the individual from the decision is important, i.e. "a bad person" vs. "a poor choice." Third, help your children understand that we can each make healthy choices for ourselves no matter what others around us choose to do. Discuss what that might look like in various situations. And, of course, it is never okay for someone to make us do something.

When was the last time someone tried to touch your body in a way that was not modest, or asked you to touch their body in a way that was not modest?

Emphasize that if this ever happens, they should tell you immediately, especially if others tell them not to. Be reassuring and calm no matter the response. This provides security and keeps important lines of communication open. Teach them they are not responsible for others' behavior.

Who are other trusted adults you can talk to when you have questions, feel uncomfortable, or need help?

While the purpose of this book is to connect parents and children, having a predetermined network of support and safety for your child is very valuable.

When you think about [situation, person, music, pictures, etc.] how does it make you feel?

Feelings and intuition are a great protection. Teach your child not to discount their feelings. Sharing your own feelings can be helpful. Additionally, if a difficult situation has already occurred (with another person, online, etc.), remember that children often share information little by little as they feel safe.

**See www.sherieachristensen.com
for additional follow-up discussion questions and conversations.**

84008013R00022

Made in the USA
San Bernardino, CA
02 August 2018